ADONICA SHAW

Forty Days of Sobriety

Practical Strategies to Break Habits and Build Stability

WINGWOMEN OMNIMEDIA

ISBN (Paperback): 979-8-2954-7283-1
ISBN (eBook): 979-8-3304-4833-3
Library of Congress Control Number: 2025926714

Published by Wingwomen Omnimedia Inc.

First Edition, 2025
Printed in the United States of America.
Part of the "Forty Days" Series by Adonica Shaw
(Forty Days to Fearless, Forty Days of Forgiveness, 40 Days of Sobriety)
Cover and interior design by Adonica Shaw.

Forty Days of Sobriety

Day 1

DECIDE WHAT YOU'RE COMMITTING TO

Sobriety begins with clarity. Before behavior changes, the decision must be specific. Vague intentions create room for negotiation later, especially when motivation dips or stress rises. Clear commitments remove ambiguity and reduce future decision-making.

This commitment does not need to be permanent or dramatic. It only needs to be defined. Whether sobriety means abstaining entirely, pausing for a set period, or stepping away from a pattern that no longer serves you, naming it creates structure. Structure makes consistency possible.

When the commitment is clear, you are no longer deciding each time an urge appears. You are simply following through on a choice already made. Today is about removing uncertainty so your energy can be used elsewhere.

Homework:
Write one clear sentence defining what sobriety means for you during these 40 days.

Day 2

REMOVE EASY ACCESS

Sobriety is influenced by environment as much as intention. When temptation is easy to reach, it requires constant self-control. When access is reduced, mental energy is preserved.

Removing easy access does not mean eliminating freedom or trust in yourself. It means acknowledging that habits rely on convenience. The easier something is to reach, the more often it will be repeated.

Early sobriety benefits from fewer tests, not more. You are not required to prove strength by keeping temptation nearby.

Reducing access shifts sobriety from a constant internal debate to a quieter, more stable process. You are not giving something up. You are giving yourself room to adjust. This is about foresight, not restriction.

Homework:
Identify one source of easy access and remove it, limit it, or make it harder to reach today.

Day 3

INTERRUPT THE AUTOMATIC PATTERN

Many habits operate without conscious thought. You reach for something before deciding to. Sobriety requires interrupting that automatic sequence long enough to regain choice.

The interruption does not need to be dramatic. A pause, a breath, standing up, or changing locations can be enough. Automatic behavior depends on momentum. Interruptions break momentum and restore awareness.

You are not trying to eliminate urges today. You are practicing noticing the space between impulse and action. That space may feel small at first, but it grows with repetition. Sobriety strengthens through these small disruptions, not through force.

Awareness creates space. Space creates choice. Choice builds stability.

Homework:
Notice one automatic habit today and interrupt it once, even briefly.

Day 4

LEARN YOUR TRIGGERS

Triggers are not failures. They are information. They show you when, where, and why urges appear. Learning them allows you to prepare instead of react.

Triggers may be emotional, physical, social, or environmental. Stress, fatigue, boredom, celebration, certain people, or specific locations can lower resistance.

Identifying patterns turns unpredictability into awareness. Sobriety becomes more stable when triggers are anticipated. Preparation reduces surprise, and surprise fuels impulsivity.

Understanding triggers is not about avoiding life. It is about meeting life with clarity. Awareness gives you options.

This is not about controlling every variable. It is about understanding your patterns well enough to respond intentionally.

Homework:
Write down one trigger you noticed today and what immediately preceded it.

Day 5

CHANGE THE ENVIRONMENT

Behavior is shaped by surroundings more than intention. Where you spend time, what you see, and who you are around all influence your choices. Sobriety becomes easier when your environment supports it.

Small changes matter. Adjusting routines, lighting, schedules, or social settings can reduce friction. You are not required to rely on discipline alone when structure can help carry the weight.

The environment does not determine behavior, but it strongly influences it. When surroundings align with your goals, fewer decisions are required. Fewer decisions reduce strain and increase consistency. You need to build conditions that make follow-through more likely without constant effort.

Homework:
Make one small environmental change today that supports sobriety.

Day 6

REPLACE, DON'T JUST REMOVE

Removing a habit creates a gap. That gap needs something else to fill it. Replacement is more effective than restriction. The replacement does not need to be ideal. It needs to be accessible. Water, movement, fresh air, conversation, or rest can temporarily replace the habit you are removing. Availability matters more than perfection.

Sobriety strengthens when urges are met with alternatives instead of resistance. Resistance creates strain. Replacement creates flow. You are giving your system a new response rather than leaving it empty-handed.

You are not just stopping something. You are building something. Over time, replacement behaviors become habits of their own.

Sobriety grows when the absence of a habit is met with intentional action.

Homework:
Choose one replacement behavior you can use when an urge appears.

Day 7

GET THROUGH THE FIRST URGE

Urges feel urgent, but they are temporary. They rise, peak, and fall. Sobriety requires learning to stay present long enough for that cycle to complete.

You do not need to defeat the urge. You only need to outlast it. Most urges fade when they are not reinforced. Experiencing this firsthand builds confidence.

Each time you ride out an urge, you weaken the pattern. The next urge becomes easier to manage. This is not about toughness. It is about patience and timing.

Sobriety strengthens through repetition, not intensity. Small wins compound. Each urge survived teaches your nervous system that you are safe without the habit.
Waiting is an action.

Homework:
When an urge appears, wait ten minutes before acting.
Notice what changes.

Day 8

BUILD A DAILY STRUCTURE

Structure reduces decision fatigue. When your day has predictable anchors, there is less room for impulsive choices.

Regular meals, sleep, movement, and routines stabilize energy and mood. Sobriety benefits from rhythm, especially in the early stages. Rhythm creates predictability, and predictability reduces stress.

Structure is not rigidity. It is support. It removes unnecessary pressure so you can focus on consistency instead of constantly deciding what to do next.
You are not limiting freedom. You are creating stability.
Stability allows growth to take root.

Sobriety becomes more sustainable when your days have shape.

Homework:
Identify one daily routine you can make more consistent.

Day 9

PLAN FOR EVENINGS AND WEEKENDS

Unstructured time increases vulnerability. Evenings and weekends remove external boundaries and increase exposure to triggers.

Planning does not eliminate freedom. It reduces drift. Knowing how you will spend unstructured time lowers impulsivity and decision fatigue.

Sobriety improves when downtime is intentional. You do not need a full schedule. You need clarity about what comes next.

Planning ahead allows you to enter these periods prepared rather than reactive. Preparedness reduces pressure and increases follow-through.
This is about guidance, not control.

Homework:
Plan one upcoming evening or weekend block in advance.

Day 10

REDUCE DECISION FATIGUE

Every decision uses energy. The more decisions required, the harder sobriety becomes.

Reducing choices preserves focus for moments that matter. Simplifying meals, schedules, clothing, and routines lowers cognitive load and emotional strain.

Sobriety is not about constant vigilance. It is about conserving energy so that when a difficult moment arrives, you have capacity left.

Fewer decisions create steadier follow-through. Simplicity supports consistency.

You are allowed to make things easier.

Homework:
Identify one decision you can simplify or remove tomorrow.

Day 11

SIT WITH DISCOMFORT BRIEFLY

Discomfort is an expected part of sobriety, especially early on. When a habit is removed, your system looks for what used to regulate stress, emotion, or boredom. The absence can feel unfamiliar, even unsettling.

Sobriety does not require eliminating discomfort. It requires learning how to sit with it briefly without immediately trying to escape it. Discomfort rises and falls, much like urges. It often feels more intense than it actually is because it is unfamiliar.

By staying present for a short period, you teach your nervous system that discomfort is survivable. You don't need to fix it right away. You don't need to numb it. You only need to allow it to pass.

This skill builds resilience. Each time you tolerate discomfort without reacting, your confidence grows.

Homework:
When discomfort appears today, stay with it for five minutes before responding. Notice what happens.

Day 12

DELAY THE IMPULSE

Impulses thrive on immediacy. The faster you act, the less opportunity there is for choice. Sobriety strengthens when you introduce delay between urge and action.

Delay does not mean denial. It means giving yourself time to regain perspective. Even short delays reduce intensity and restore clarity. What feels urgent often loses power when it is not acted on immediately.

By practicing delay, you weaken the habit loop. The impulse no longer guarantees a response. Over time, impulses become less commanding because they are no longer rewarded automatically.

Delay builds self-trust. You learn that you can pause without collapsing and choose without pressure.

Homework:
Practice delaying one impulse today by at least ten minutes before deciding.

Day 13

DON'T ROMANTICIZE THE HABIT

Romanticizing a habit keeps it alive. Memory has a way of editing out consequences while highlighting relief or pleasure. This distortion makes sobriety harder.

Sobriety requires accuracy. The habit served a purpose, but it also came with costs. Ignoring those costs reinforces longing. Seeing the full picture restores balance.

This is not about shaming yourself or demonizing the habit. It is about remembering honestly. When the habit appears attractive, gently recall what it actually delivered over time. Clear memory supports clear decisions.

Homework:
Write down two costs of the habit you are stepping away from, without judgment.

Day 14

SEPARATE WANTING FROM NEEDING

Wanting something does not mean you need it. Urges often blur this distinction. Sobriety strengthens when you learn to separate desire from necessity.

Needing implies survival. Wanting implies preference. Most urges fall into the category of wanting, even when they feel intense. When you recognize this difference, urgency softens.

You are allowed to want something without acting on it. Desire does not require fulfillment in order to pass. When you stop treating wants as emergencies, pressure decreases. Sobriety becomes more stable when urges are seen as temporary experiences rather than commands that must be obeyed. You gain flexibility and choice.

This distinction restores proportion. Not everything that feels strong is essential.

Homework:
When an urge appears today, label it clearly as a want rather than a need.

Day 15

TRACK WHAT ACTUALLY IMPROVES

Early sobriety can feel uncomfortable, which makes it easy to overlook progress. Tracking what improves helps balance perception and sustain motivation.

Improvements are often subtle: clearer mornings, steadier energy, better sleep, improved focus, or fewer emotional swings. These changes matter, even when they don't feel dramatic.

Without tracking, discomfort can overshadow progress. Writing improvements down creates evidence that the effort is working. Evidence builds confidence.

Sobriety strengthens when benefits are noticed intentionally rather than assumed. Progress is cumulative. Tracking helps you see what would otherwise be missed.

Homework:
Write down two specific ways your life feels more stable, clear, or manageable since starting.

Day 16

EXPECT RESISTANCE

Resistance is a normal response to change. When a familiar habit is removed, the system pushes back. This does not mean the decision was wrong.

Expecting resistance reduces surprise. Surprise fuels doubt. When resistance appears, you can meet it calmly instead of questioning your commitment.

Resistance may show up as irritation, restlessness, rationalization, or fatigue. Naming it reduces its influence. You don’t need to argue with it or eliminate it.

Sobriety stabilizes when resistance is anticipated and tolerated rather than feared. Resistance often fades when it is not engaged.

You are not failing when resistance appears. You are adjusting.

Homework:
Notice one way resistance shows up today. Name it without acting on it.

Day 17

HANDLE SOCIAL PRESSURE

Social pressure can complicate sobriety, especially when habits were shared.

Comments, expectations, or subtle cues may create discomfort.

You are not responsible for managing other people's reactions. Sobriety is a personal decision. Keeping explanations minimal preserves energy.

Planning responses in advance reduces anxiety. Neutral, simple statements prevent negotiation and reduce stress.

Sobriety becomes easier when social situations are navigated intentionally rather than reactively.

Homework:
Write one short response you can use if questioned about your choices.

Day 18

SAY NO WITHOUT EXPLAINING

Saying no can feel uncomfortable, particularly if you are used to accommodating others.

Sobriety requires practicing refusal without justification.

Explanations invite negotiation. Boundaries are clearer when they are brief.

You do not owe anyone a detailed rationale for protecting your stability.

Each time you say no without explaining, self-trust strengthens. Sobriety becomes less fragile.

Homework:
Practice saying no to one small request today without offering a reason.

Day 19

STOP TESTING YOURSELF

Testing yourself can feel like proof of progress, but in early sobriety it often creates unnecessary risk. Placing yourself in tempting situations to see if you can handle them keeps the habit active in your awareness. It asks your nervous system to perform under pressure before stability has fully formed.

Sobriety does not require constant demonstrations of strength. Strength is built quietly, through consistency and reduced exposure. Each unnecessary test drains energy that could be used to reinforce new habits and routines.

When you stop testing yourself, sobriety becomes less effortful. You are no longer negotiating with temptation or proving resilience. You are simply living within structures that support the decision you've already made.
Protection creates progress.

Homework:
Identify one situation, place, or interaction that functions as a test. Choose to avoid or modify it this week.

Day 21

PROTECT EARLY PROGRESS

Early progress in sobriety is both valuable and delicate. The changes you are making are still settling, and stability is still forming. Protecting this phase is not about fear. It is about care.

Protection may look like simplifying your schedule, limiting stimulation, maintaining routines, or saying no more often than usual. They are temporary supports that allow momentum to build.

Progress compounds when it is protected. Each steady day strengthens the foundation beneath you.

This is not the time to overextend or prove how much you can handle. It is the time to reinforce what is working and remove what threatens it. Protection now creates freedom later. You are building something worth protecting.

Homework:
Write one specific action you will take this week to protect the progress you've already made.

Day 21

NOTICE MENTAL CLARITY

As sobriety settles, you may begin to notice changes in how your mind feels. Thoughts may arrive more cleanly. Decisions may feel less tangled. Even if clarity comes and goes, its presence is worth noticing.

Mental clarity does not mean constant focus or the absence of stress. It often shows up quietly, as fewer racing thoughts, less internal debate, or a greater ability to stay with one idea at a time. These changes are subtle, but they matter.

Sobriety reduces background noise. When the mind is not occupied with managing or recovering from a habit, attention becomes more available. That availability supports better judgment and steadier emotional responses.

Noticing clarity reinforces progress. It reminds you why the effort matters. Clarity grows through consistency, not perfection.

Homework:
Write down one moment today where your thinking felt clearer or more settled than before.

Day 22

STABILIZE ENERGY AND SLEEP

Sobriety often affects energy levels and sleep patterns before anything else feels different. Early changes may be uneven. Some days you may feel more rested. Other days may feel flat or restless.

Stabilization takes time. Your body is adjusting to new rhythms without the habit it once relied on. Consistent sleep and wake times, regular meals, and reduced stimulation support this adjustment.

Sobriety benefits when basic physical needs are prioritized. When energy and sleep stabilize, emotional regulation improves and urges often soften.

This is not about optimizing performance. It is about creating steadiness. Steadiness supports everything else. You are allowed to rest more than usual during this phase. Recovery includes recalibration.

Homework:
Identify one small adjustment you can make tonight or tomorrow to support better sleep or steadier energy.

Day 23

MANAGE STRESS DIRECTLY

Many habits functioned as stress relief. Removing them exposes stress that was already present. Sobriety requires learning how to manage stress directly rather than through avoidance or numbing.

Direct stress management does not need to be complex. Movement, breathing, rest, and setting limits all reduce stress when practiced consistently. Addressing stress early prevents it from accumulating into overwhelm.

Sobriety becomes more stable when stress is acknowledged instead of ignored. Ignored stress often resurfaces as urges. Managed stress loses intensity. You are not required to eliminate stress. You are learning to respond to it differently. That skill develops gradually.

Managing stress directly builds confidence. You learn that you can handle discomfort without relying on old patterns.

Homework:
Identify one current stressor and one direct action you can take to reduce its impact.

Day 24

AVOID SUBSTITUTING ONE CRUTCH FOR ANOTHER

When one habit is removed, it is common for another to try to take its place. This can show up as overworking, overeating, excessive scrolling, or other forms of avoidance. Sobriety includes noticing substitution patterns early.

Replacing one crutch with another delays learning how to tolerate discomfort directly. Awareness prevents this from becoming automatic.

This is not about eliminating all coping strategies. It is about noticing when a behavior functions as avoidance rather than support.

Balance matters. Sobriety grows stronger when relief comes from sustainable practices rather than new dependencies. Awareness keeps substitution from becoming a new habit loop.

Homework:
Notice one behavior today that might be functioning as a substitute. Write it down without judgment.

Day 25

STRENGTHEN SELF-TRUST

Each sober decision builds self-trust. Over time, trust grows not from perfection but from consistency. You learn that you can follow through even when it feels uncomfortable.

Self-trust develops gradually. It is reinforced each time you keep a commitment, pause instead of reacting, or choose long-term stability over short-term relief.

Sobriety restores confidence that may have been eroded by broken promises to yourself. That confidence extends beyond the habit itself.

Trusting yourself makes future decisions easier. Doubt decreases. Internal negotiations shorten.

Sobriety is not only about removing a habit. It is about rebuilding your relationship with yourself.

Homework:
Write one example from this week where you followed through despite discomfort.

Day 26

PREPARE FOR BOREDOM

Boredom often appears when a habit is removed. Time opens up. Stimulation decreases. This can feel uncomfortable at first.

Boredom is not a problem. It is space. Sobriety requires learning how to tolerate and use that space rather than escaping it.

Preparation helps. Simple plans, low-effort activities, or intentional rest reduce the urge to fill boredom impulsively. Boredom often signals adjustment.

As your system recalibrates, new interests and rhythms emerge.

Allow boredom to exist without immediately fixing it.

Homework:
List one simple, neutral activity you can use when boredom appears.

Day 27

EXPECT EMOTIONAL FLUCTUATION

Emotions may feel uneven during sobriety. Some days may feel calm. Others may feel irritable or heavy. This fluctuation is normal.

Habits often dampened emotional range. Removing them allows feelings to surface more clearly. This does not mean emotions are worsening. It means they are becoming more available.

Expecting fluctuation prevents alarm. When you anticipate emotional shifts, you are less likely to interpret them as failure.

Sobriety stabilizes over time as emotional regulation improves.

Patience supports adjustment.

Homework:
Notice one emotional shift today without trying to change it.
Write what you observed.

Day 28

STAY CONSISTENT, NOT PERFECT

Sobriety does not require perfection. It requires consistency. Small, repeated choices matter more than flawless execution.

Perfection creates pressure. Pressure increases strain. Consistency allows flexibility while maintaining direction.

You will have uneven days. That does not erase progress. What matters is returning to the path without self-punishment.

Sobriety becomes sustainable when expectations are realistic.

Progress grows through repetition.

Homework:
Write one way you can prioritize consistency over perfection this week.

Day 29

LEARN FROM SLIPS WITHOUT SPIRALING

If a slip occurs, response matters more than the event itself. Spiraling into shame increases risk. Learning restores stability.

A slip is information, not a verdict. It reveals where support, preparation, or boundaries may need adjustment. Responding calmly preserves momentum.

You can acknowledge what happened without abandoning the larger commitment.

Sobriety strengthens when mistakes are met with curiosity rather than judgment.

Homework:
If you've had a slip, write one thing it taught you. If not, write how you would respond calmly if one occurred.

Day 30

REINFORCE NEW HABITS

By now, new patterns may be forming. Reinforcement helps them stick.

Repetition, structure, and recognition strengthen habits over time. What you repeat becomes familiar.

What becomes familiar becomes easier.

Sobriety stabilizes when new behaviors are reinforced intentionally rather than assumed to stick on their own.

You are building something durable.

Homework:
Identify one new habit you want to reinforce and one way you will support it this week.

Day 31

REDEFINE YOUR RELATIONSHIP TO CONTROL

Sobriety often changes how you think about control. Many habits existed as attempts to manage feelings, stress, or uncertainty. Removing them reveals where control was outsourced rather than practiced.

Sobriety is not about rigid self-control. It is about intentional choice. Control becomes less about forcing behavior and more about directing attention, time, and energy with clarity.

You are learning to tolerate uncertainty without immediately trying to regulate it away. This builds a quieter, more sustainable form of control that does not depend on constant effort.

As sobriety deepens, control shifts from reaction to leadership. You are no longer responding automatically. You are choosing deliberately.

Homework:
Write one way your relationship to control feels different now than it did before.

Day 32

BUILD A SOBER IDENTITY

Sobriety eventually becomes part of how you see yourself. Identity shapes behavior. When sobriety is integrated into identity, decisions require less effort.

This does not mean labeling yourself or announcing change. It means quietly recognizing who you are becoming through repeated action. Identity grows from consistency, not declaration.

A sober identity is flexible. It adapts without rigidity. It supports choices without pressure.

As this identity forms, temptation loses relevance. You are no longer deciding what to do. You are acting in alignment with who you are.

Sobriety stabilizes when identity catches up with behavior.

Homework:
Write one sentence describing who you are becoming through sobriety.

Day 33

CHOOSE LONG-TERM OVER IMMEDIATE

Sobriety requires choosing long-term stability over immediate relief. This choice becomes easier with practice, but it still requires awareness.

Immediate relief is tempting because it promises quick comfort. Long-term benefits arrive more quietly. Sobriety teaches patience with outcomes that unfold over time. Each long-term choice strengthens confidence. You learn that delayed rewards are reliable. Trust builds.

This is not about denying pleasure. It is about aligning pleasure with sustainability.

Sobriety grows stronger when you choose what supports tomorrow, not just today.

Homework:
Identify one recent moment where you chose long-term benefit over immediate relief.

Day 34

REDUCE RELIANCE ON WILLPOWER

Willpower is limited. Sobriety becomes more stable when it relies less on effort and more on structure.

Reducing reliance on willpower means simplifying choices, maintaining routines, and protecting energy. These supports reduce strain and increase consistency.

Sobriety thrives in systems, not struggles. When fewer decisions are required, follow-through improves naturally. This is not about becoming rigid. It is about becoming supported.

Sobriety strengthens when willpower is reserved for moments that truly require it.

Homework:
Write one way you can reduce reliance on willpower this week.

Day 35

CREATE ONGOING GUARDRAILS

Sobriety is easiest to maintain when it is supported by guardrails rather than constant vigilance. Guardrails are the structures, limits, and routines that prevent unnecessary exposure to risk. They are not about fear or restriction. They are about preserving stability.

Guardrails might include consistent schedules, limits around social environments, reduced access to triggering situations, or clear boundaries with people who unintentionally undermine your progress. Their purpose is not to shrink your life. It is to protect the parts of it that are growing. You spend less time negotiating with yourself and more time living within conditions that support your decisions. This makes sobriety feel less fragile and more integrated.

Stability needs reinforcement before it becomes self-sustaining.

Homework:
Write down two guardrails you want to keep in place for the next month and why they matter.

Day 36

NOTICE WHO YOU ARE BECOMING

Change is often difficult to see while it is happening. Sobriety works quietly, reshaping habits, reactions, and self-perception over time. You may not feel dramatically different, but you may notice increased steadiness, clarity, or follow-through.

Who you are becoming matters as much as what you are stopping. Sobriety restores parts of you that may have been muted or postponed. Confidence grows not from feeling strong, but from watching yourself act consistently in moments that used to feel difficult.

Noticing these changes reinforces progress. It helps your mind register that effort is producing results. Without this awareness, growth can be overlooked and undervalued. Identity shifts through repetition. Each sober choice reinforces a version of you that is more reliable and more self-directed.

Homework:
Write one quality in yourself that feels stronger or steadier now than it did before you began.

Day 37

PLAN FOR THE NEXT 40 DAYS

Sobriety is not an endpoint. It is a practice that continues beyond a defined timeframe. Planning ahead prevents drift and supports continuity once the structure of these 40 days is complete.

Planning does not require a rigid blueprint. It requires awareness. What worked? What created strain? What conditions supported consistency? Answering these questions allows you to move forward with intention rather than uncertainty.

Without a plan, progress can feel temporary. With a plan, sobriety becomes portable. You carry the lessons forward instead of leaving them behind with the calendar.
This is not about committing forever. It is about deciding what comes next. Direction matters more than duration. Sobriety strengthens when momentum is extended deliberately.

Homework:
Write one specific intention for how you want to support sobriety over the next 40 days.

Day 38

KEEP IT PRACTICAL

Sobriety is most sustainable when it remains practical. Overcomplication creates pressure, and pressure increases risk. What works is often simple, repeatable, and realistic. You do not need elaborate systems or constant self-monitoring. You need routines that fit your actual life. Simplicity reduces friction and makes follow-through easier, especially during stress or fatigue.

Practical sobriety focuses on what consistently works rather than what sounds impressive. It prioritizes function over theory. When sobriety fits into your day without requiring constant attention, it becomes durable.

Complexity can feel productive, but it often masks avoidance. Practicality supports stability.
Keep what works. Let go of what doesn't.

Homework:
Identify one part of your sobriety routine that can be simplified without losing effectiveness.

Day 39

PROTECT THE GAINS

The progress you have made deserves protection. Sobriety creates gains in clarity, energy, and self-trust. These gains can be maintained with intention or lost through neglect. Protection does not require constant effort. It requires awareness of what threatens stability and a willingness to respond early. Small boundary adjustments now prevent larger disruptions later.

Protecting gains may mean continued routines, reduced exposure to high-risk situations, or ongoing limits around stress and stimulation. These are not signs of fragility. They are signs of respect for what you've built.

Progress compounds when it is protected. Sobriety becomes less about recovery and more about maintenance.
Value what you've earned.

Homework:
Write one concrete action you will take to protect your progress over the next month.

Day 40

CARRY SOBRIETY FORWARD

Sobriety is not something you complete and leave behind. It becomes part of how you make decisions, manage stress, and relate to yourself. What you've practiced over these 40 days is a skill you can return to when needed.

You now have evidence. You know what it feels like to pause, choose deliberately, and follow through. That knowledge does not disappear when circumstances change. Carrying sobriety forward does not require rigid rules. It requires awareness of what supports clarity and what undermines it.

You are equipped to notice the difference.
Sobriety becomes less about abstaining and more about alignment. It supports the life you want to live rather than limiting it.

You are not finished. You are prepared.

Homework:
Write one sentence describing how sobriety will continue to support your life moving forward.

About the Author

Adonica Shaw is an entrepreneur, medical device innovator, doula, and author whose work spans women's health, design, and leadership. She is the founder and CEO of Wingwomen Technologies Inc., Wingwomen Omnimedia, and Shaw Surgical Innovations LLC, companies dedicated to redefining women's experiences in healthcare and business.

She is the author of What No One Tells You About Motherhood, Disrupting Delivery, and Natural Birth Control, with additional titles across wellness, leadership, and women's personal development. Through her writing, Adonica offers grounded wisdom and emotional clarity to women navigating growth, ambition, and self-trust. Her work reflects a deep commitment to helping women build lives and companies worthy of their vision.

www.ingramcontent.com/pod-product-compliance
Lightning Source LLC
LaVergne TN
LVHW051131210926
848482LV00001B/63
* 9 7 9 8 2 9 5 4 7 2 8 3 1 *